AF303992

Maher Asaad Baker

Silver Land Ballads

Contents

Introduction

Music in Argentina has energetic music that has captured and assimilated its music into Argentinian society. The majority of folk music forms that described the regional division of Argentina were located in the vast territory of this state. From the joyful notes of the Andes to the sensual notes of the Pampas one can notice that music has been the voice of Argentina a long time ago.

Regarding the people of Argentina, music is not only an art; it is that art that defines people and compels them to embrace the chronicle of their nation.

It is for that reason that Argentinian folk is about everything that people have to deal with in their lives, and has been narrating it through its melodies for years. The dances include; the sad milonga and mournful, zamba which inclines to love, chacarera—fecundate of joy and so on and the aspects of emotion it covers are love, loss of a loved one, joy and the like. The themes are based on the real life of ordinary people of Argentina mostly struggling with poverty, political strife and so on. Hence, folk songs involve people's perception and in return provide a voice to many who can otherwise not be heard. In this respect, they preserve the image of the people with a certain rather raw naturalism that has no equal.

It thus remains a positive correlate of the rite of customs in Argentina with a bidirectional relationship. For instance, there is such a musical rhythm as the Malambo which can be characterized as rather classical and at the same time inspired – it is used in the wild and vengeful dance called the Malambo, which is performed at the folk festivals. The last elaborate event prior to the Lent season is carnival; there are magnificent dancing and music shows, that involve salsa and samba. Other fragments of religious culture also have folklore elements, e.g., Catholic processions accompanied by bagpipe and drum music. In both of these examples, the 'novel' or 'Gili' is used to create the spirit in all celebrations irrespective of its elaborateness in Argentine society. From this perspective, all these practices of folk music have at least some references to some events of some past generations and hence they are beneficial.

However, folk music in Argentina has intrinsic cultural importance; however, it benefits from institution. In Argentinean schools, music and dance are part of the learning curriculum so that children are taught education in music right from their initial years at school. Other forms of local music groups are also sung in the communities where the preserved Argentine folk music is taught to the young generation by the elders. They have the aim of maintaining really valuable types of folk music within the tendencies of globalization. Thus, the culture and tradition of the earlier generations remain in Argentina societies in as much as the songs and sounds are inherited from one generation to the other.

Argentine music can be viewed as the origin of a link for a state that is so heterogeneous. Other folk genres that have also emerged in the territory of Argentina are equally welcomed as people's property and something impossible to ignore when talking about the incipience of the story belonging to all the Argentines.

Despite the fact that every region of Argentina has its distinctive timbre, it is possible to state that there is only one unifying thread running through the entire culture of this country – the desire to take up an instrument and begin to play on it. But songs as simple as those that emanate from the remote parts of Argentina are always considered to be part of Argentina folklore even with some of the songs origin dating back to indigenous or foreign origin. When the migrants took their instruments as well as dances to the cities, forces in the urban societies were crossbred. Argentine folk genre was, therefore, made from all these forms of music that were characteristic of the region. This has meant that through music, the diverse cultures in a country that in one way or another is very diverse has been able to find a common ground.

This is how the socio-cultural change has always impacted on the political periods in the history of Argentina in as much as folk music is concerned. The New Argentine Song of the 1960s–1980s are political protest songs contrary to the mainstream that led to the rebellion of the Argentine citizens against the military dictator. Such passionate and such powerful words turned into the songs of the fight. Regarding the present day, other political activities including poverty and human rights also provoke traditional music. Since freedom and equality are related to the people, for the most part, Argentine folk music, and social justice issues have a song.

Differences in culture and geographical characteristics of the Argentine territory contain a wealth of various types of folk songs that, firstly, are different depending on the region. Paired indigenous wind and percussion elements of Huayno music derive from the northern Sierras or Andes. Payada is marked by reciting ballads typical for gaucho cowboys of the Pampas grasslands. The Colombian immigrants brought into the northeast their cumbia dance tunes. The following are some examples showing how regional folk genres negotiate individual characteristics of the locals in Argentina. Globalization on the other hand is a force that attempts to unify musical dialects and merge them, attempts at preserving musical dialects are ways of making sure regional identity and culture are not dormant.

The omnipresence of music in daily life confirms Argentina's status as a musical nation: tango beats in Buenos Aires streets, carnival rhythms in hot and wet provinces, and sting sounds of bagpipes in the cold vastness of the south. In this concert of which each rumor is the note, it is possible to distinguish the spirit of the Argentine people. The brief given here paints only a rudimentary picture of the culture that forms part of this kaleidoscope and is so huge. But it is that, which even refers to the Argentino style of folk music, is the ability to convey the experienced emotions – both good and bad – at a pitch higher than the linguistic. These songs remained forever preserved in the loving heart and through it closed a past that adds nutrients to the heart of Argentina.

Argentine Music Origins

The music of Argentina is such a lovely and diversified tune that has blended with different agencies of the society due to diversified periods of history. If one wants to look at the roots of Argentine music then one has to turn towards the lens to early colonial days and the meeting ground of the Euro-Indian cultures. This synthesis of these musically different sectors rendered new avenues of rendition that define Argentina's music at present. Analyzing the historical and cultural backgrounds of this kind of interaction allows obtaining information about the development of Argentina's music and its impact on modern music.

European colonization of the area in the 16th Century brought the seeds of massive transformations to the current Argentina music. European colonizers especially the Spanish and Portuguese brought together with them musical instruments and styles that were very easily adopted by the people of the region. The guitar, violin, and harp which were formerly important musical instruments in the Americas region, began to assume new importance in the new transformation of the musical productions of the region. These European instruments, which were backed up by the new techniques, merged thus with the indigenous rhythms and melodies to produce what can be termed as the new cultural music.

From the colonial masters, therefore, came a substantial impact on the local music traditions. The Spanish and Portuguese authorities thus imposed on the Indigenous people their taste in music, which in turn were clearly articulated into tropes of formalism and aesthetic structures that would have been alien to them. These changes in the European way of doing things caused the slow assimilation of these features into the already existing indigenous ones. The fusion of the musical forms became a symbol of the rich and rather contradictory social and political context of colonialism and its effects on the arts.

Having combined both indigenous and European cultures the catholic church had an influence on the musical culture in Argentina. During colonial times the Church was one of the most important centres and sponsors of art and the main driving force behind the development of various forms of music. This they achieved through the introduction of choral music and religious compositions which were so predominant in the earlier years. Religious institutions such as churches and cathedrals also emerged as primary makers and concertizing spaces of music, that was sung in worship and festal events.

Sacred music was used for religious education as well as for entertainment. Other forms of music also emerged in Argentina: for example, the Gregorian chants, polyphonic choral works and hymns were transplanted and transformed in Argentine soil to feed into the evolution of the Argentine liturgical music genre. Through these compositions, not only did the devotees have a medium of worshiping God but, the transitioning music culture was enriched with European music assimilation thereby influencing the subsequent music culture of the region.

reciprocally, the work of imperialism reveals the interpenetration of European and Indigenous contrariness in the formation of new musical forms and genres in Argentina. Native music, oriented on the native instruments like the drum and flute and the rhythm, gradually incorporated new elements from European music like, for instance, disharmony and melodic lines. These two formed a blend that generated new musical genres that were a mix of the original cultures of the area and the colonial masters.

One of the most important consequences of this integration was the creation of traditional Argentine genres like 'chacarera' and 'zamba'. The chacarera which is still a folk dance with a fast tempo also has indigenous rhythms and melodies of European origin. In the same way, the zamba a slower still and less syncopated dance than the tango incorporates European harmonies with Indigenous musicality. These genres are an allegory of the synergy of different traditions and they are also a proof of the innovation and versatility of Argentine music.

Music is also deemed to have served social and cultural functions in colonial Argentine society. Art was a way of communication for different social standards and ethnic backgrounds, showing their objectives and feelings. Consequently, Indigenous people of the region used music as a means of maintaining a culture and, thus, an identity in the face of colonial pressure. To the Europeans and the accepted social stratum, music provided a way of sustaining culture and announcing social standing.

Not only, the combination of different musical components, as well as the emergence of new types of music were not only the masters' desire to experiment but also ousted by social and cultural realities of the epoch. Thus, some aspects of colonial society were represented in music as freedom, people's identity and power relations. The new musical forms that emerged were both the signs of their cultural integration as well as resistance which clearly directed how music could function between cultures and within the changing cultural paradigms of the given period.

Thus, over time, new types of Argentine music developed, which differed from each other in connection with the geographical and cultural characteristics of this or that region of the country. Musically in Andean the use of wind instruments and complicated rhythm was usual while in the Litoral region, music was based on the accordion and lively beats. This required music that was in sync with the life and culture of the Pampas region which included grasslands for cattle and large open tracts of land for grazing, which is home to famous who are known as gauchos and other related forms including milonga.

These regional musical styles were therefore, in part, defined by geography and climatic conditions. For instance, the Andean highlands developed a tradition of wind instruments and high-pitch melodies out of the altitude character of the region. Whereas the more monotonous geography of the Pampas influenced music with a more beat-response, because of the plains and the life of the country's cowboys. These differences helped to give the various regional forms of Argentine folk music their character and speak again of the relationship between setting and music.

During the early periods of Argentina's folk music, several important personas that contributed to the development of folk music also preserved and developed the traditional folk song and music forms. Many of those wonderful artists were folk musicians and composers who naturally blended the Indigenous and European musical traditions: Atahualpa Yupanqui is a vivid example of this. His role in establishing these two styles of music: chacarera and zamba is expositionary of the fact that these styles are part of the most significant of Argentine Music.

Another giant of culture was Carlos Gardel who contributed to the development of Tango and took this kind of music to the world stage. While tango's birth is associated with the working-class migrants of Buenos Aires, Gardel played a role in the process that upgraded it into the formal, international type of Argentine music. Bernardo gave an innovative approach to integrating both European and local music and thus was instrumental in shaping the future sound of the Argentine tango.

These early composers, and performers not only maintained putting into practice the traditional music but also modernized them, thereby making them remain fashionable and relevant. It could be stated that thanks to their work, the further development of the musical culture of Argentina was stimulated, and the modern diverse palette of the musical tradition of the country described how important the early sources and the tendencies evoking their echoes in further evolution.

The beginnings of Argentine music are therefore the sign of the elaborate intertwining and evolution of cultures during the colonial era. The fact of the interpenetration of European and Indigenous cultures in the process of colonization and with the impact of the Catholic Church created the basis for the formation of styles and musical genres. Of course, over the decades and centuries since the birth of Argentine folk music, the genres and artists also introduced regional differences and personalities to the already complex mix. Knowledge of these origins is interesting in terms of understanding the diversity of Argentine musical legacy in view of the historical and cultural development of the country.

Folklore

Argentina is among the Latin American countries with rich cultural origins; its conventional folk music includes assorted territorial melodies as well as dancing. From the cheerful, folk-pop chamamé of Corrientes to the melancholic tangos and milonga of Buenos Aires, the Indigenous, black and white populations of Argentina have had an unequal and over time, diverse cultural experience. Concerning the most representative and popular varieties of Argentine folklore we can mention the zamba, chacarera, milonga, and chamamé. They all differ in their attributes while all of them participate in the construction of the nation and national identity.

Zamba

Of course, the zamba is one of the most popular and typical Argentine rhythms which may be regarded as the second national anthem although at present Argentina has no national song. Zamba emerged during the colonial period of the Viceroyalty of the Río de la Plata where Indigenous rhythms mixed with sucks and chants of Latin America with Spanish tunes and string instruments. It stretched its existence for quite a number of centuries to continue enhancing the complexity of its framework, including such aspects as, for instance, African polyrhythm including those that were added at the earliest stages of the twentieth century that can be associated with tango.

The first Zambas were descendants of the Andean culture in the present provinces of Jujuy, Salta, Catamarca and La Rioja and Tucuman in the northwest province of Argentina. It also moved eastward across the country in the mid-19th century when a phase of immigration from northern Argentina after the Wars of Independence crossed the country. Part of the regional variations were evolving while others remained the same, and the musical parameters and the dance components were fixed. Zamba songs are love songs that mostly talk of love, waiting, sorrow, nature, country and whatnot, all these sung to guitars, Bombo legüero drums, charangos, queens and other Andean wind instruments.

From a dance perspective, Zamba is typically performed by couples and those who dance 'couple dance' make use of smooth touches sometimes suggestive of courting. It is in Zumba, while still not particularly flashy and quite demure, the woman spins under the man's lifted arm several times at a figure called vuelta quebrada literally translates as 'broken turn'.

Besides folkloric shows, the term ~amba was introduced to the large public through other practices of the performing arts that inclined towards popular culture or with new artists who altered the idiomatic structure of this genre. These are the Nueva canción musicians such as Mercedes Sosa and Atahualpa Yupanqui who revolutionized the political and stylistic direction of Argentine folklore since the fifties with emphasis on such aspects as voicing of social issues in the lyrics and incorporation of aspects of Western pop into the music. Being, in some ways, the most versatile of all Argentine folklore music and dance types, Zambia's cultural function is likely to shift in the future.

Chacarera

As a dance that originated from the folk tradition prevalent in the rural Sierra of Northwestern Argentina, it is generally associated with the Chacarera music representing the 'gaucho' kind of cowboy culture associated with mestizo peasants of Santiago del Estero, Tucuman, Catamarca, Jujuy and Salta. The origin of the genre is thought to be in the first half of the twentieth century, however, the full incorporation of the charango, kensho and even piano into a typical lineup of guitars and bombo legüero drums played with hands, happened.

Nevertheless, other aspects of chacarera are the instrumental support of the songs and the rhythmic structure of the 6/8 and 3/4 metric conflict. There is a pulsive rhythm that simultaneously appears in two distinct units, which together create vibrancy and movements, sharp dynamic rhythms ranging from 170-200 BPM at times. Therefore, chacarera necessitates a fast couple dance referred to as 'Zapateo' and involves high-speed footwork, spinning, kicking, stamping and leaping traditionally performed on rustic earth or wooden floors which represent the rural areas and fairs.

Some of such Chacarera groups and singers like Los Chalchaleros or Roberto 'Changüí' Barboza initiated in the 1940s thus establishing the Chacarera and its utilitarian value in the Argentine folklore. Further, in the next decades, it proceeded to expand its popularity and impact through other important artists like Mercedes Sosa, embodying this kind of style in her shows together with the progressive shifts originating from mainstream folk and folk rock conventions. As a whole, modern chacarera's arrangements move from simple to complex with optional brass or synthesizer parts but still with a bombo legüero drum set as a central component.

Milonga

It is important to underscore the fact that it is very frequently misconceived as a sub-genre of the Argentine urban tango style of music known as 'tango milonga' In fact 'milonga' as a style is completely different and actually originated in the Argentine countryside, or 'campo', and predates the tango. Milonga is best traced back to the peoples of the Río de La Plata's interior, during the middle of the 19th century. Although the genre was cheerful guitar music linked to the gaucho festivity and dancing in the beefy countryside of the nation, the initial form of the milonga was very different from the gradually developing, piano-based tango of Buenos Aires of the early twentieth century.

This, however, sets Milonga apart from Argentina's famous tango relation though they share a distant related stock. The later half of the 1800s saw boys from the countryside bring the fast milonga guitar rhythms into the porteño social dancing and over the years, they impacted the evolution of the metro area's tangos through what came to be known as "tango milonguero". As tango was just beginning the Golden Age which commenced about 1920 and 1930, the sharp separation of the two was already accomplished while milonga's higher rhythmic energy remained as a faint reminder of its lineage which would warp tango further into a complex and developed cosmopolitan art in the following years.

In contrast to tango which might have been derived from the African influences based on the rhythm which is analysed in the paper, milonga can be viewed as having a completely different origin, first of all because it differs from tango in many ways starting with the fact that it is danced to music with an accentuated upbeat tempo which is somewhere between 120 and 240 beats per minute. Guitars are also much louder in the milonga, while other instrumentations of the classic orchestral tango are dominated by the bandoneon. Lyrics also help to distinguish the two as milonga has more rural themes and lyrical playfulness that is characteristic of rustic stories; the lyrics are sung in the so-called triste or baguala song genre.

In terms of the nature of performance practices for the milonga, this is ranked from singers to conjunto and further up to full orquesta típica where the basic structural elements such as guitars and accordions might be augmented from time to time with string basses pianos or other percussive instruments. Vocally, a special feature is singing while the interpreter performs on an instrument in his hands, as the interpreter is similar to a one-man band. As for the second position, the couples perform the milonga using an effervescent movement pattern, including steps, kicks, taps, and spins suitable for the energetic types of music.

Over the years since its inception, the milonga has taken root in other forms of contemporary society through fusions that contain its dance rhythm while presenting varied forms and styles; from the engine of Argentine rock to electro-milonga techno remixes or a dramatic play. All these are based on the dance rhythm of the milonga. As such, milonga is an actively practiced musical genre that has taken shape and is still in the process of doing so from several centuries of rural tradition; at the same time, it remains open to the processes of cultural change.

Chamamé

Chamamé: animated music that emphasizes the multicultural character of the Mesopotamia region of Argentina with a focus on the provinces of Corrientes, Misiones, and a part of Entre Ríos. Stylistic components can be regarded as features of indigenous Guaraní cultures, additional features of sub-Saharan African cultures with whom the Jesuit missionaries came, European (particularly Spanish) instruments that were introduced by the colonizers, and accented ports played from the neighboring regions of Brazil. The genre was defined by the mid-twentieth century century also including other formats such as polkas which even sound different from chamamé styles in even further south locations such as Buenos Aires.

From an instrumentation standpoint, chamamé is mainly played with a button accordion, guitar and bass guitar as main instruments and Guaraní rainstick percussion as part of the combination, together with violin, mandolin, wind instruments or casual, simple light striking of the cajóns or woodblocks as accessories. They range from slow, even balladic and up to the frantic dance tempos of around 160-200 bpm. Thus chamamé offers assistance to various interpretive gestural expressions starting with listening to music up to dancing with sliding movements, trotting like walking, hopping or shuffling in quadruple time for a tempo that is fast.

Concerning its content the lyrics vary from romantic ballads to lyric poetry, the themes may concern nature, rural life or social life in the area. The second independent melodic line, which is sung, is the human voice which in chamamé music is as important as the rhythm and the instruments and is usually performed in an expectant and yearning style. This is in accord with the cultural role of the genre of helping to retain the northern Argentina/Paraguay 'community' and also the expatriate 'community' in other countries retaining its deep cultural connection to chamamé music through generations.

Chamamé rise to national fame was between the period of 1950s to 1970s through such artists as Argentinian folk music icon Ramon Ayala, groups such as Los Paraguayos and Los Nocheros and artists such as the accordion-playing Chango Spasiuk who also revived interest in chamamé playing more contemporary styles of the music. The present-day chamamé and the next generation and other musicians have also helped in the preservation as well as in the reinvention of chamamé through artists like Victoria Birchner, Bruno Arias, Lorena Blanco and many other prodigies who have taken chamamé to other level of the 21st century.

Argentine folk is a blend of regional music; a beautiful rug that has been woven with the different colored yarns. From the sensual and dramatic Zamba to the vigorous and sweet Chacarera, from the innocent and cheerful Milonga, and joyful and lively Chamamé, every music genre has its own story to tell about Argentina. These musical traditions are not mere entertainment; they are assertions of people's cultural realities, past and presence.

Tango

Tango is also described as a "feeling that is danced." is an intense and stylized dance created from 1880 through 1902 in the area known as the "barriada" of Buenos Aires, Argentina and Montevideo, Uruguay. Originally it was concocted from African, Argentine and European roots and in the course of the following one hundred years it evolved into one of the most famous and significant elements of Argentine folklore.

In its turn, tango is a cultural phenomenon that implies specific types of music, poetry and, most critically, dramatic dance. As history or as dance, tango is about saying goodbye, grieving, suffering, and desire in the context of love. The fast and complex rhythm, the close embrace and partner dance, and the lyrics of tango as a form of expression depict the forbidden love that Argentines have in them. It started in Buenos Aires, the Argentine port city now associated with the people of Buenos Aires or the 'porteños'.

Tango appeared and was formed during the early twentieth century and slowly and steadily moved to Europe, the United States and other parts of the world. This was to become one of Argentina's most famous cultural exports. Currently, tango is a constantly evolving dance, people are trying to adopt tango to the contemporary world adding the popularity of such forms, keeping the passion, the

Historical side of the dance born in the barrios of Buenos Aires.

In the middle of the nineteenth century, the growth of the population of Buenos Aires was registered by immigration. Europeans came to Argentina in the hope of improving their living standards and fleeing poverty and wars, Africans on the other hand came as slaves in the early days until the mid 19th century when slavery was abolished.

These different groups coexisted in Buenos Aires, and the contact that was made between them generated transformations and recombination of the music. The salon-style dances that were born from the waltz and polka moved and merged with the intricate rhythm of the candombe drums of the African peoples. Candombe had departed with the

African slaves across the Atlantic and its rhythm was already beating in local districts. To this was added the sad songs of milonga danced by gauchos and country hicks seeking work in the city.

It was out of this union that tango emerged in the 1880s in the working class port areas of Buenos Aires such as La Boca with a large European flavor and San Telmo – the black area of Buenos Aires. Here the tango was spontaneously created by people, it started in their conversations, it grew in the narrow and confined tenement yards and it evolved progressing from one generation to the next.

It was in the early twentieth century that this style developed into what was referred to as the Brazilian Tang which was already popular in Paris before it was taken back to Buenos

Aires. Argentine Tango then borrowed from this style improving the footwork and the shapes of Argentine Tango. Impressive dancers of tango of that early period like Rosendo Mendizabal amazed spectators with this, and as such, created a basis for the needed interest in tango.

Some might wish to opine that tango could only turn into a proper professional dance after Café El Parisien opened its doors in the year 1912. Drawing its premise from the Monserrat neighborhood located in downtown of the city, El Parisien gave an atmosphere of afternoon tango show and dance classes. For those recipes, the complement of rich people would come to take classes and, besides, communicate with the dancers of this town. Tango's popularity boomed.

Slowly, theatres on Corrientes Street proper became almost entirely specialized in professional tangos. The Buenos Aires authorities tried to control the dance tango and prohibited women from dancing this type of dance insisting that it was too erotic and rather vulgar. Of course, attempts were made to stop the spread of the dance only to strengthen further the understanding that tango had indeed become a part of the popular culture. This continued to change out of the port side neighborhoods to be the spirit of Buenos Aires.

Tango at this time was synthesized with other distinct music styles but quickly managed to develop a distinct style of its own. Through fusions between European meters and African ones, the new rhythms appeared and one of the areas one could point to them is the rural folkloric genres such as the milonga. The early versions in which tangos were written were the manuscripts that were in circulation orally especially up to the first scores of the early part of the twentieth century.

And already for the year 1930, it is already possible to speak about tango music as such, its Golden Age. Tango was danced precede by orchestras típicas, which was a collection of musicians who mostly included violins and guitars. Largest inside it had been the bandoneón, strictly translated from Spanish as 'big accordion,' although it was imported by the German as well as the Italians and was the shrill, moaning voice of tango.

Especially, the bandoneón does not discard the sadness and the affection that is the essence of the tango dance. In an Orquesta, there is a bandoneón instrument and strings, and telling stories of tragedies, passion and regions of Buenos Aires; there is a narrative singer. All the songs are musically developed using two staff parts and each of them boasts of a set phrase; the flow of the dance content is all about the lyrical content of the song. Here the rhythm pattern is the downbeat with the syncopation added to indicate where the accents lie being on the offbeat. Dancers also threatened a bet on the beat or with something in anticipation of the syncopation, with the intention of being dramatic.

Tango orchestration developed through key bandleaders involved being them being Julio de Caro and Juan d'Arienzo mainly in the 1930s and the 40s. The tango is becoming more lyrical, and D'Arienzo is going to start a fast pace that will in the future be called tango fantastico – very dancing, or at least no whining. This was a line between the traditional and the liberal within the trade that composers have been keen on drawing up to this point.

Ástor Piazzolla late in his career went back to the Tango and that is when he included counterpoints to his music but they were modern counterpoints using basic elements of tango and other devices. Moreover, within the course of creating a cultural artifact, tango contains new stimuli in its structure, such as piano jazz and electronic music, so it preserves its mnemonic function. However, in any case, with regard to the fact that tango is considered to be kitsch or posh, it is important that tango retains the Unicode feeling, and people get interested; meanwhile, the leaders of the tango couple can add flaps to the songs.

It was because the dance involved more than simply touch that the scandalous movements related to tango were present from its inception in the 1880s. I remember that at the time we had a completely different attitude to the division of sex and transportation of women and men. However, the closeness offered everyone to get to another stage where he could be as frank as he only was on the dance floor.

During the dance people embrace each other with the upper part of the body, the chest part of the body. In a leader's role leaders use several sensations and movements to guide their partners across the choreography and that includes steps, kicks, sweeps, and ganchos (legs hooks). This makes each dance look like an improvised dialogue of the leads as they try to give the interpretation of the emotions as narrated in the music.

By the 1900s Competitive Stage tango, was at its peak and people flocked to cafes and theatres in Corrientes. Choreographers added fouettes and individual interpretations of the dance had made the dance spectacular with an athletic and sexual appeal. This inspired the crowds given that the people got to see and experience love and affection between people.

While attempts were made to restrict the dance at the beginning the tango spread to all levels of the porteño society. The attempt to enforce pious conduct exhausted the opportunities for constructing a strict moral code, but instead, it reaffirmed the imaginative function of tango in freeing a frustrated emotion and in forging a relationship with the dance partner.

Starting from the outdoor terraces of the first-generation immigrants' dwellings and moving up to the marvelous stages of the city's theaters, tango became an inherent part of the Argentinean ethos. It is tempting as it gives one chance to be weak and close – to embrace such timeless concepts as penetration and subjection, surrender and ostentatiousness that shape people's lives. Tango is built on the very basic and perhaps the purest feelings that any person has within.

The tango was taken internationally by Argentine dancers who started giving performances in Europe and later some of them including Juan Peron went to Paris and shocked them with accurate and passionate beats. High society adopted the dance which was made more interesting by variations in body posture like the upper rigid part of the body and the free lower part down to the feet, Parisian steps included.

From French tango, body dissociation and fast poses which are less improvisation were included. The prompts for the introduction of theatrical styles that performed in Teatro came from influential actors such as Carlos Gardel also known as "The King of Tango", an Argentine celebrity based in France. The flaming tango spectacle was created through exotic dance shows that first interested people abroad, and later locally, in the early 1930s and 1940s.

In the following decades, the popularity of Argentine tango goes up all over the world. Among the dances that were danced by the dancers and were imported back to Buenos

Aires were the salon tango and the American ballroom which included new technicalities. But in the 1980s and the 90s tango entered Europe with the musical and the dance revolution of Pov Piazzolla. Finnish Tango, however, did so in the manner that styles did in other countries, whereas Argentine took more highly inventive and tightly clutched forms.

And tango continues invading borders in the twenty-first century. The so-called contemporary advances in tango including tango nuevo or tango fusion encompass new and complex steps as well as new changes in the pattern of the rhythm of tango. They are still kept alive by the dancers from Tokyo to Tehran owing to the traditions that grew in the barrios of Buenos Aires.

It supports the global tendency that Tango is the way to get people – with passion against words or cultural barriers. In other words, tango is not actually a dance of complex floor work, of high and fantastic lifts, but of dominance and submission, of hopelessness and happiness. It is that feeling in terms of emotion that is emitted from the heart of Buenos Aires.

And if there is one man who is most identifiable with the tango, then it has to be the man they called the 'Knight of Song', the singer and songwriter, the man who was also an actor – Carlos Gardel. Francisque Gardel was born in Paris in 1890 but, since early childhood, he was growing up in the Abasto district of Buenos Aires; he is considered one of the prototypes of the tango singing, the poet owner of the velvet voice and the overwhelming expressiveness. His tunes such as "Mi Buenos Aires Querido" and "Por Una Cabeza" for which words were written by Alfredo le Pera are sung completely from the heart by tango lovers of Buenos Aires.

However, Gardel is gone too soon by drowning his singing career in a plane crash at his peak in 1935. His death therefore transformed him into a cultural icon of Argentina which people in this nation and other parts of the globe grieved over. But the recordings of Gardel are vivid examples of tango's dramatic and sentimental temper that still stirs people's hearts while being 80 years old.

The second force that further contributed to the development of tango was Ástor Piazzolla, an Argentine bandoneónist, and composer, who took the leadership of tango's development in the 1950s and attempted to integrate jazz and classical elements into tango. Francesco was recognized as the founder of the Nuevo Tango; indeed, he altered the style of the tango and the manner in which it was played whilst using the Quinteto Nuevo Tango, nonetheless, he conserved the spirit of the music.

Among them, there are "Libertango" or Four Seasons of Buenos Aires (Cuatro Estaciones Porteñas) which belong to the so-called nuevo tango. He won a Grammy award for his compositions; his works took tango from the streets into international concert halls but were not well received by tango purists. Both Gardel and Piazzolla also took this music and danced it into the next generation and the eternal soulfulness.

Alongside the key symbols, there is the list of people – musicians, poets, and dancers who left their imprint on the history of tango. Working-class themes were represented as sensations of poetry in the souls in the lyrics of the late Celedonio Flores after which there were early composers comprising Eduardo Arolas, Juan de Dios Filiberto and Agustín Bardi.

Juan D'Arienzo was the one to provide the tropical, lively swing in the dance orchestras of the 1930s, and which continues to seduce the milongas. Even at his age as a young bandoneónist, Piazzolla's imagination was caught by Anibal Troilo who used harmonic and melodic Counters with ostinatos to give the sensation of rhythm. The dancing of Carlos Gavito and Juan Carlos Copes on Broadway and films started taking tango around the world in the 1980s after the

Argentine military junta sought to suppress the art.

In the new millennium, others who developed nuevo tango dance grammar include Gustavo Naveira and Pablo Verón while on the music side, Daniel Binelli made sure that Piazzolla's music and ideas lived on by continuing to play them with his Orquesta Típica Julián Araña. But, in fact, the list does not end here; with campeonato salon dancers and ending with jazz innovators of electro tango. Both have left the soul of Buenos Aires in the continuous construction of tango in the world.

Tango emerges from African drums washing the European coast; from orchestral violins embracing Gardel's deep voice to Piazzolla's electric band performing concertos; from tenements' patios where parents pass the dance's beat – the generation breeds the generation in tango. The creativity continues today. Tango is not an invention to be credited to one artist but an art that springs from the shared tradition of the people.

Tango is a debate between two individuals; two people are encouraged to hug to touch each other's souls. That is the tradition that was brought to the Buenos Aires barrios in 1800. It will always be a way to go home to the neighborhoods that helped to bring the dance into existence. Today, however, tango remains the pulse of the city and sends a message that each of them should make the author of this magnificent creation.

Rock Nacional

Rock Nacional or Argentine rock emerged in the 1960s-1970s as a vigorous and has become a significant rock and youth culture that reflected the problems of the generation that was growing up in the time of political crisis. borrowing at the same time influence of the rock music from the international scene, rock nacional, bands and artists in Argentina had started to form their own direction, channeling their songs with themes that youth could associate themselves with, the frustration and optimism of post-revolutionary period was portrayed in the songs. With the evolution of teenage magazines alongside the evolution of the political context of the country, rock nacional was much more than songs – it was the voice of a generation trying to find its identity in years of defiance.

Before the 1960s, Argentina's popular music hardly boasted of anything more than folk and tango. In initial, rock music started getting its basic base in of 1950s when American and British rock singles and LPs entered the country. Regarding the early Argentine bands, for example, Los Gatos and Almendra, the Anglo-American hits were translated, and they introduced their performances in songs by Presley, Beatles, Rolling Stones and other bands of the same directivity. This foreign musical influence together with a growing youth culture was the premise for the emergence of Argentine rock.

Late in the 1960s there bands like Los Gatos composed and performed Mexican rock and roll songs and thereby began the rock nacional. That is why the genre could develop – Argentina was experiencing a growth of urbanization and a new young middle class was being formed. University students became politically active and noisy protesting against authoritarian government. Argentinian middle-class youths in the seventies and eighties saw rock coming out of England and the US as having something to say about life under tyrannical regimes. This spirit and energy were moved by local bands into a new music form that was to be known as Argentine Rock.

In the subsequent ten years, the movement took form as new bands were formed and the recording industry was created to accommodate new talents. It could be said that the British New Wave progressive rock group Invisible was the first to achieve this kind of success in the early seventies with a series of successful albums. Other distinguished bands were Pescado Rabioso, Vox Dei, Sui Generis, La Máquina de Hacer Pájaros and Arco Iris which recorded a blend of music with flavors of rock and other subgenres such as jazz tango folk blues and classical. They ranged from as far as the music itself and as near as the bands' lyrics in Spanish that Argentine youth could understand.

By 1972 another wave of albums pointed out that rock nacional was not only the music of a subversive counterculture in Argentina but also of a country in a moment of revolutionary transformation.

It was therefore the presence of rock music in other countries which was then taken to Argentina and interpreted in Spanish and translations of the lyrics were produced which were understandable to the bands. The early inspiration was derived from the rock 'n' roll stars of the 1950s like Elvis Presley, Chuck Berry, and Little Richard and from the British Rock bands of the 1960s like The Beatles, The Rolling Stones and The Kinks.

Rock Nacional went on to the 1970s and like the British the Argentineans started listening to progressive and psychedelic bands Pink Floyd, Genesis, Yes and King Crimson through bands of Latin Rock such as the Invisible, Espíritu and Contraluz. Heavyweights like Led Zeppelin, Deep Purple and Black Sabbath also made their influences felt in the recordings of Argentine power trios Pappo's Blues and Vox Dei. Working with artists such as bassist Pedro Aznar and drummer Oscar Moro, the so-called house band style was a very jazzy and eclectic sound, based on the influences of Santana, Chicago and Weather Report which are all jazz fusion bands. Rock nacional emerged through inspiring other artists for example folk artists like Dylan, Young and Baez on folky deeper groups like Sui generis or artists like Litto Nebbia & Gieco Leon.

In addition to musical influences, the Argentinian rockers emulated other avant-garde aspects of the international rock process – Townshend and The Who burning his guitar, Hendrix burning his guitar, the spectacular Pink Floyd and so on. Argentine bands embraced international rock imagery and music at the same time that they engaged in the development of a rock-centered identity in Spanish, as did rock movements in other parts of the world.

As the music of the Argentine youth, rock nacional was an element of the process, associated with the essential social change processes. A product of the 1960 this genre saw the emergence of middle-class youths in the country who ranted about issues to do with art censorship, freedom of politics and corrupt military rule by Juan Carlos Onganía. Rock Nacional carried growing frustrations and calls for a change in society.

In the 1970s political instability rose and the violence between the right-wing-focused government and leftist guerrilla stepped up and in 1976 Isabel Perón was removed from power by the military. Democratic rule was thus succeeded by one of Latin America's most oppressive military juntas. For the military, Argentine youth and rock bands were the first to feel the crackdown since they were viewed as possible subversives. Concerts were forbidden, artists detained or expelled, and the powerful movement of rock nacional born in the beginning of the 70s was violently suppressed.

While the situation in Argentina deteriorated from 1976 to 1983, some of the most repressive years in the country's history, societal and political topics receded slightly from rock nacional songs. But the actual music continued to tease political messages in coded form amidst the lyrics of its songs. The new wave contained synthesizers and drum machines for earlier rock instruments and the topics will be loneliness in the city and survival under dictatorship. Although not as noisy, rock nacional persisted in defining the youth subculture and dissent.

Rock Nacional was already in the process of being reprised as soon as Argentines transited to democracy in 1983 following the Malvinas War. In homage to what has been made, Sui Generis and Serú Girán reunited in concerts in 1987 and 1988, and generation groups like Los Fabulosos Cadillacs were preparing the rock to recover the role of protest music. Rock Nacional had shown that rock & roll was as vital as ever and that the attempts of regimes to silence the generations of young Argentine people through their music were not successful.

It was used in the military dictatorship to name actions taken against the ruling power as resistance.

Rock Nacional was considered a greater threat since it was the most dominant form of music through which freedom of speech was being exercised when Argentina was under right-wing military dictate from 1976 to 1983. The new regime thus set out on a violent crackdown campaign known as the Dirty War it targeted political dissidents – the death or disappearance figure might range up to 30,000. Having no civil rights, Argentine society saw itself oppressed and living in the aura of governmental violence.

When it came to rock nacional artists pinpointed as subversives from the onset, the punishment was severe. The rock stars including Gustavo Santaolalla and Luis Alberto Spinetta had to disappear into hide. Another musician and performer, another charismatic singer-songwriter Litto Nebbia was imprisoned for a year and later escaped abroad too. And the very promising folk-rock band M. I. A was kidnapped and did not bring out another album. Steinvils's corpse was identified only when its skeleton was almost decomposed after his disappearance in 1978, and he was a legendary musician from Argentina named Edelmiro Molinari.

For those rock bands who nevertheless carried on recording – albeit tentatively – during the Dirty War, compromise was inevitable. They did not often explicitly discuss repression, disappearance, or death that would work as propaganda against the regime. There was the use of prose and poetic language with many devices such as the use of the following objects: fear – persons in isolation, and full submission to the dictatorship.

As public concerts were limited, some rock nacional artists connected with the audience by playing for a few people in people's houses, making the performances seem like secret shows. Some brave bands such as V8, a hard rock band, went on recording rebellious songs such as "Brigadas Metálicas," regarded as subliminal anti-dictatorship songs. Although totalitarian authority had sharply limited Rock national's prior development, its essence remained boiling as the emblem of youth personality and rebellion.

One of the most important bands of the 70s of Argentine rock was the folk formation Sui Generis, formed by the guitarist Nito Mestre and the pianist Charly García. Four studio albums released between 1972 and 1975 consist of acoustic ballads and orchestral rock addressing existential concerns of youth. High concentration on music and lyrics which can be compared to progressive rock guitarist Robert Fripp.

When Sui Generis disbanded in 1975, the outrageously gifted García formed the jazz-rock band La Máquina de Hacer Pájaros and later, in 1976, Serú Girán. Transforming sorrow for the disappearance of friends into four elaborate, ambitious, virtuosic rock albums under the military regime, García was nicknamed "El Príncipe" (the prince) and "El Profeta del Rock" (the prophet of rock). His canonization at a concert in 1980 gave testimony to the fact that he was unique in shaping the identity of Argentine rock. Serú would keep recording until García ventured out on his own in the '80s as democracy emerged.

In 1985, an inspiring vocalist Carlos "Toto" Ferreira started a ska band Los Fabulosos Cadillacs. Combining reggae, funk, rap and rock, Sandersismo is their 1990 work that marked the rock nacional back with protest sense, cheerful songs and parodies of old corruption bipartists. Los Fabulosos Cadillacs introduced a new fresh energy and a stage presence that fascinated audiences around the globe making Argentine rock popular again.

Some of them are records which tell moments of the Rock Argentino history. The mix of poetic lyrics and the rock and roll sound indeed characterized Almendra's 1970 debut album, self-titled. Pescado Rabioso released their second album Desatormentándonos in 1972 which bore testimony to a stormy pinnacle when rock dared to enter the live music arena. El jardín de los presentes (1976) by Invisible is the quintessential example of avant-prog rock's bourgouis intellectualism just before the repression. Los Twist: the 1983 LP La dicha en movimiento signaled rock nacional rising again along with liberated society. The album Divididos por la Felicidad published in 1984 by Sumo is a well-crafted marriage of punk rock aesthetic and regional South American rhythms and sumptuous lyrics that are still relevant today; it delves into existentialism. Soda Stereo's 2007 mega concert album Ruido Blanco revolunteered stadium crowds to the band's rock nacional on the verge of exporting their music as a cultural commodity.

Of all the most legendary – Moris' 1970 anarcho-punk 'El Oso' some consumers named vandal linked consumerism with vatic rhetoric that empowered a generation. With "Sudamérica O El Regreso a la Aurora", 1972's metaphysical mega hit Arco Iris proclaimed that rock is fated for social justice. On the album "La Colina de la Vida" released by PorSuiGieco in 1976 the guitar tunes conveyed the sorrowful loss of friends that have disappeared as the thousands of people felt could relate to the song. In the song "No te enamores nunca de aquel marinero bengalí", produced in 1982, Los Abuelos de la Nada presented a metaphorical view of a society under dictatorship and the problems of the idolatry of the authorities. Riff's Elemental 1984 number 'Solo quiero rock and roll' had an angry feel that was a sign of the rebirth of rock n roll. And there is still the pathos coming out of "Flaca," Andrés Calamaro's bitter ballad of spleen from 1999, which explained why, through the political and economic changes of the years, the poetic spirit of Argentine rock has stayed alive for those who seek redemption.

Starting with rock and roll in the 1950s and the counterculture movement in the 1960s, Argentine rock repurposed globalized artistic importation into a charged politicized youth rebellion against repression and liberation. In its rebellious lyrics and unconformist sound, rock nacional has been for decades the soundtrack of the new generations confronting oppression cycles. Its growing collection and sustaining ethos defy the trials that Argentines have faced as they pursue democracy: It is important to learn how to get knocked down and then get up again. Bursting out into the new millennium, democracy restored, the inexorable cry of formative rock nacional records still resonates – the living testimony of the Argentine youth in the age of light as proved by this compilation even amidst the country's grim dystopia of violence and apprehension in the specified period. But in the middle of all of that, rock nacional is the only real and sincere musical passion of the Argentine people.

Cumbia

Cumbia is a beautiful dance of Colombia that has spread in most of the South American countries depending on the impact of the regional culture in each country. Cumbia has not entered as deeply into any country throughout the world as much as it has into Argentina. Argentine cumbia or cumbia villera originated in Buenos Aires' shantytowns and then spread like wildfire to penetrate all over Argentina crossing all classes. It has since risen to become the uncontested people's music or the music of the populace. It is this dance music in 4/4 time with guitars and accordion and drums prevailing and at times wind instruments provided the tamborito beat all through the arrangement. Of cumbia, as for the latter, it has something to do with the destiny of the subalterns of Argentinian society, that, nevertheless, makes all the Argentines dance.

Cumbia is a Colombian dance that originated with the African population in the Atlantic coast area of Colombia, the dance is a type of courtship dance that has indigenous, African and Spanish influence. The traditional cumbia ensemble consisted of chonta drum, flutes, vocalists and the key instrument: the tambor alegre (happy drum) with which the music of the genre presents the distinctive shuffle rhythm. As this new form of cumbia began to spread inward from the coast of Colombia and beyond It created regional variations of its instrumentation, rhythmic and vocal structures.

It is said that initially in the 1940s and 50s, some records of Colombian cumbia were brought into Argentina and the working-class inhabitants of the squalid barrios of Buenos Aires took it up. These separated and often stigmatized populations of people could identify with the emotion-laden lyrics of cumbia which was about hardship and loss. Popular local bands then started to produce more cheerful numbers of Colombian cumbia, while Argentine musicians started to compose new cumbias using the low-prestige Buenos Aires patois called Lunfardo. Colombian rhythm and Argentine working-class lyrics fused and created something new on which modern cumbia villera has been built.

This emerging genre was only audible in the villas miserias until the late 1990s when bailanta dance parties were linked to middle to upper-middle-class youths and then through TV personalities who gave the music their endorsements. Other decades brought different local Argentine developments of cumbia where other instruments like the electric guitar, drums and keyboards started to be included. There are also some musical peculiarities typical for most dance music styles, including Argentine cumbia: The role of drums is more emphasized For all this, there appear some differences between Colombian and Argentine cumbia, such as more elementary and suitable for munchos chords progressions. The tempo was then reduced once more for the Argentine tango-like dance that was being depicted. Lyrics began to incorporate other facets in life, and not only the complications of life, but love, regions, soccer teams, and such. Once the means of communicating out of the limelight for the marginal, this has evolved into Argentina's dance music per excellence across the divide of the strata.

In Buenos Aires, the new variation called cumbia villera or shantytown cumbia was beginning to evolve and became well known in Argentina. The instruments that characterize cumbia villera are now the electric guitar, bass guitar, keyboard, and a bombo legüero drum. As for Colombian cumbias, they are noted for complex rhythm and playing of a variety of percussion instruments; villera, in contrast, is fast-paced and involves minimum use of chords played on strings, enough to allow the couples to dance. Songs contain typical working-class stories or those that include the usual parlance.

As cumbia villera the music has social implications because it stemmed from the lower stratum of society and spoke for the subjugated class. A good example is the use of vigorous language involving crime, drugs and sex which the middle and upper classes dislike. Moreover, the popularity of the genre also complements the fact Argentines are not as divided by class as is sometimes believed. On the same note, it deploys the struggles of the villa, even as this has a fast beat, it unites Argentines of all classes to dance to cumbia villera.

It became that way when cumbia was moved to the foreground as the pop music of Argentina, and subgenres arrived. Cumbia romántica (romantic cumbia) comprises tunes with depressive or sweet messages or love songs. Tropical cumbia consists of processes like the Puerto Rican salsa. Fusión subgenres add rock, reggae, reggaeton, electronic and many other styles to cumbia. Present-day evolutions include infused or programmed cumbia beats with steamy voices and guitar. purist resurgence has also been pointed out as contemporary bands attempt to look for lost early Villera recordings.

Cumbia, therefore, is not yet static but still expands instrumentally as well as in the lyrics to reflect the Argentines. While cumbia was once the music of the disagio, of the margins, of the borderlands, it has become the dance music of Argentina's heartland.

Los Wawancó are the precursors of the cumbia sound of the original sixties mix of Colombian cumbia with Argentine spices. Their first hit single 'Monedita de Oro' helped kick-start the trend of mainstream use of

Buenos Aires working-class creolle language in songs sung to the rhythm of cumbia.

Pablo Lescano started it in the early 1990s through his band Flor de Piedra and he is, indeed, the godfather of cumbia villera music enjoying the maximum number of crossovers in his genre. Through making slang descriptions of the marginalized life, Lescano made cumbia available for everyone to consume. Songs like "Me estoy acostumbrando" brought Cumbia Villera into the light and into the billboard.

After Flor de Piedra, with Damas Gratis Lescano at the head of the genre, cumbia villera was the most representative style of music in the year 2000. Their biggest hit ever "Me Vas a Extrañar" had a melodic form as well as the lyrical form which addressed such issues as crime and forgiveness. It was considered the face of the new representation of Argentine cumbia to the low pedigree and high prestige classes.

The rock and roll have been incorporated into cumbia by Los Palmeras. Their song 'La suerte está echada' combines the power chords of the electric guitar with the Mexican accordion which is an example of how cumbia assimilates modern music.

Thus, while early bands like Los Wawancó pioneered Argentinian cumbia in the process of translating working-class Spanish into the danceable rhythm of Colombian two-step and contemporary groups like the aforementioned Damas Gratis who popularized the aggressive and kind of tough cumbia villera for the generations of today, contemporary bands ensure cumbia music for the next generations.

The seemingly lowly barrio origin of cumbia elevates it to the apogee of the current taste, a microcosm of the Argentine character. Its festive rhythms bring equalization to a dance floor regardless of the status of the people in the society economically. As tango is danced in the basic neighborhood dance hall, cumbia unites all Argentines through happiness, and music, and dance. No longer can it be regarded as mere music that was produced with the intent of making the people dance; it is the beat of the Argentine nation.

Festivals and Celebrations

Argentine celebrations and performances are as blended as the roots of the country – indigenous peoples intervened here Together with Europeans and Africans, as well as the gauchos of the Pampas region. Yearly such occasions offer the chance to inhabit a historical, arts, and community exploration of Argentina.

There is also a great number of festivities, occurring in the country, and one of the most popular is the Buenos Aires Tango Festival that is annually held in the capital city in

August. This festival attracts thousands of dancers and enthusiasts from different parts of the world showcasing performances, workshops, and milongas of tango is the official dance of Argentina. The last activity of the festival is the World Tango Championship show where the most excellent dancers engage in a battle for the title.

The carnival that takes place in February is another vivid celebration that is on Argentina's list. The carnival of Argentina is not as famous as that of Brazil specifically Rio de Janeiro However what is up north is as colorful. Cities such as Gualeguaychú become the sites for parades, Costumes, and tunes that hover between African and 'indigenous' drums. The festivity involves dancing and singing including what is referred to as Murga, this is a theatrical event typically performed in the streets and which presents a number of social themes.

Other folklore festivals are; Inti Raymi for winter solstice and Pachamama Raymi for the god of the earth in the Andean area. In August the above one is celebrated for fertility where food items are taken and offered to the landslide goddess called the Pachamama so as to bring fertility and hence good harvest. There are dances and music in connection with the festival and demonstrated enactment of the indigenous people's ritual in which stress is laid on people's relations with nature only.

Other festivals of Modern Gaucho culture such as Fiesta Nacional de la Tradición were established in San Antonio de Areco. Observed in late November, this festival is a simulation of the gaucho through horseracing, Wilfrido, Polo championships, and music. It is a good chance to receive the actual idea of Argentine pampas, which are free from the influence of Europeans or any other type of population.

Yet another aspect that is characteristic of the culture of Argentina is that of festivals of a religious nature. Fiesta de la Virgen de la Candelaria is celebrated in February in the northwest region of the country; the dance has Catholic origins but has assimilated Indigenous influences. It means there are parades, as well as music and dance, ruffles and other performances that depict the very core of the religious rituals in Argentina – a mixture of Afro Spiritualism and Catholicism.

It can be said that these festivals and celebrations are not only the production and reproduction of Argentina's culture but are also the creation of unity and nationalism. Both the residents and the tourists are encouraged to enjoy the several cultural activities that are offered in the country, making Argentina one of the most culturally intense countries to visit to enjoy the festivals.

The Feria Nacional del Matambre is a yearly event held in the town of Gonzalez Catán, Argentina and like the latter; it is in terms of size a city located near Buenos Aires. It is also known as the 'Capital of Matambre,' a thin cut of beef that is often used in Argentinian dishes. This typical food is taken on the festival and it pulls the locals and tourists through musical, dancing and culinary troupes and other cultural displays.

The event is celebrated in November for four days hence the title Feria Nacional del Matambre. It is relied upon by more than fifty thousand visitors annually, with Argentines as well as internationals. It was set up in the 1960s to promote the sale of cattle and meat, including beef products of Argentina. It started changing over the years into a colorful affair where people presented food and music and other things they consider as part of the endowment of the region.

Among the enjoyable elements of the show is preparation, especially the large portions of matambre which is grilled over charcoal and sold in sandwiches. Feria in 2007 produced the largest matambre sandwich for a record having a length of more than 300 feet. The people of Chile include these dishes with people attempting to produce the largest or the most uniquely wrapped matambre dishes.

There are also the paintings and sculptures of locals, the place for children to play and the tricks associated with Argentinian cowboy 'gauchos.' Every day folk singers and dancers perform on few stages made for the territory of the fair. But most importantly, it brings the guests of the Feria in contact with the traditions and culture of Argentina.

There are a number of songs and dances associated with the Feria Nacional del Matambre. It also presents artists from all the provinces of Argentina, who show the local music and dances of the country.

Probably the most often observed dance at the festival is the Zamba dance. Zamba is a dance originating from the countries of the north of Argentina and is typified by dancing for couples to music with the use of guitars. Though prettily dressed, and brightly lit with colorful décor that portrays ethnic wear, both the partners have their feet moving as fast as their hands; through tapping and Heel clipping while in a hold.

Argentine people perform entertainment including the dances like chacarera and escondido, which are found in the pampas grasslands of Argentina. Fast solos and duet or group hand-in-hand dancing is also found in the chacarera, as well as the rhythmical manipulation of scarves. The dramatic escondido includes several aspects of the act of hiding, and courtship, or flirting with looks and gestures.

The Feria also celebrates the plain Argentine music styles of chamamé for an area near Paraguay and bolero for North Argentina. It also has a feature of polka style of rhythm that involves accordion, and harmonica, guitars with dancers moving in pairs on the dancing floor. In Bolero groups it is combined guitars, tambourines, and indigenous, African and European components are compounded in the melodies.

Besides the tango show and the delicious meat, guests of the Feria Nacional del Matambre can also enjoy music and dancing from different regions of Argentina. In a way, the festival becomes a miniature representation of the cultural diversity of Argentina.

One of the oldest and most significant cultural events in Argentina is the annual Cosquín Folklore Festival. Established in 1961 in the small mountain town of Cosquin in the central Córdoba province, the festival was created in order to gather performers of folk music from across Argentina after a folk concert broadcasted nationally from the town the previous year proved immensely popular. The Cosquín Festival, which runs for nine days in January and February of the year, has grown over the past sixty years as the principal festival for Argentine folk artists and audience members interested in rustic, Indigenous music and dance including chamamé, chacarera, zamba and many others.

As a result of the concert of the prior year, the first Cosquín Festival was attended by approximately 15000 people as well as key Argentine folklore artists upon the start of the festival in 1961. Since then, the festival has remained a ground to help new artists from the region gain popularity among the masses. visitor turnout is now well over 200,000 per day of the event. It has grown into a three-day event with three main musical arenas, a shop full of local artwork and crafts, numerous food vendors, and a ride and game zone for children.

In addition to the exhibition of performances, the festival's purpose places special emphasis on the dissemination of genres that are part of the Argentine folk canon. Through the years great artists of Argentine folklore, such as Mercedes Sosa, Atahualpa Yupanqui and Los Chalchaleros opened their careers or commenced their professional activities again being captivated by the audience of Cosquín. In the 1990s, this festival was adding a more modern flavor to the traditional style of music and making the young generations of the nation aware of their roots back on the farms. Cosquín today offers a platform for legendary folk artists to mentor the next lot and also increase the scope of the genres.

It is worth taking into consideration the fact that the Cosquín Festival has been a gathering of almost all the legendary musicians of Argentinean folk music since its inception more than sixty years ago. This was quite common in the 60s and 70s when soloist Mercedes Sosa graced the stage to seal her place as one of the vanguards of Argentina's folk songs. Another bright and solitary testament that comes from a solo artist, this time a guitar player, is to Horacio Guarany.

Influences and Exchanges

It can be argued that people all around the globe know music as they breathe in and out since it breaks all barriers and encompasses all divides of cultures, states, and oceans. This truth resonates well in Argentina, a country whose musical traditions of tangos, cumbias, and other music forms have not only incorporated foreign elements in the course of a century but also can pride themselves on having an impact on the world.

Another characteristic of Argentine music is that the lines among all those genres are blurred, and elements from several forms of dance music are combined. Tango, which was first of all prominent as a mixture of European, South American, and African musical traditions, developed in parallel with jazz and rock, but folk or music combined pan-Latin American instruments. In turn, crossover superstars from everywhere have done the reverse commute to Argentina to record in other genres. Likewise, native talents — tango artists such as Carlos Gardel and Astor Piazzolla, and singers of rock en español like Gustavo Cerati and Charly Garcia — have brewed artistic revolutions elsewhere.

The penetration of the international scene in the music is interpreted as a result of the diversified cultural roots of Argentina. There were two large immigrations in the second half of the nineteenth century and the early twentieth century, and Buenos Aires became the melting pot into which most of the foreign music styles were assimilated and adapted. These overseas imports merged with rural traditions over several decades into characteristic hybrid styles for Argentina. It is not only tangible exchanges in the form of band tours and studio recordings that have made an almost palpable impact on the country`s production of art. In turn, Argentina has also taken its music to the world stage. Orchestras of tango started visiting Europe more than ninety years ago. The ensembles took the audience by storm because they improvised classical–tango fusion. Bands of Rock Nacional, leading figures of counterculture in Argentina throughout the 1980s, managed to leave their mark as far north as Mexico and as far south as Chile. These indie genres have currently conquering the world through music streaming since they made their way across oceans. As the culture opens up bit by bit with the help of technology,

Argentine music will hopefully remain relevant in the world for many more years.

In that sense, the course of development for Argentine genres was underway with various tendencies in world music, from the first forms of jazz through to current hip-hop. At least, this seemed to be the case a century ago when direct artist-to-artist borrowings and more distantly inspired sounds from afar made their way into tango, Argentine rock, folk, and even classical music. Indeed, the most famous ensembles of Buenos Aires and campesino musicians entering this period did ensure that there was a continuity of local practices through new syntheses with features from elsewhere.

From tango, which was itself a product of the bordellos and bars of European immigrants in the 1850s, to the mass diffusion of rock Americana in the 1960s, and the so-called modern pop of the 21st century—foreign influence reached almost all forms of Argentine music. Specific bilateral relationships inspired creative works or made known foreign demand for its artists. As noted, if means of transport and communication are still both under construction, so also are there manners in which the music belches across the outback borders into Argentina.

Dramatic Tango The dramatic tango song form has its roots way back to mid-nineteenth-century Buenos Aires where aboriginal, European, South American, and African rhythms merged in the developing port districts of the capital. Most writers divide the history of tango into three large periods: the so-called first period—the guardia vieja—from approximately 1850 to 1920, and it can be considered as the birth of the tango in this cosmopolitan area; the second one is the period of the guardia nueva, between 1920 and 1955, where tango started its way towards internationalization; the last one is the so-called post-guardia nouveau, which started during the 1950s and could be considered as tango that has been influenced by the modern world.

At its formative stages, it was European immigration that fueled tango. The Lumpenproletariat and the Italian and Spanish people fleeing poverty and military service used the same port of Buenos Aires; male immigrants dancing at bars created the basis of Tango's machismo; arm movements are borrowed from flamenco. It was early tango, inherent with African influences like syncopation and Cuban-like call-and-response vocals, which developed in the lower areas of

Buenos Aires before starting to rise in mainstream popularity in 1909 when it performed at the Opera Theater.

It was in 1917 that tango was widely associated with proper bands or orchestras, such as when jazz swing came in from North American horn musicians traveling to Argentina. While the Tango craze internationalized abroad, it continued to fan further fusions at home. It was in Paris in the 1920s that classically trained musicians began to use jazz instrumentation in tango composition, really opening the way for Argentine composers like Piazzolla to continue even deeper these musical investigations.

For the entire history of tango, it's international collaborations that have sparked the very excitement of the genre. Native Argentinian, Creole Latin jazz piano virtuoso Lalo Schifrin gained an international audience; classic tango nuevo legend Piazzolla released two albums with American jazz musician Gerry Mulligan in the 1970s and constantly toured around the globe until his death in 1992. Among other modern Guardia vera EP standouts are Argentine-Swiss Tanghetto with tango reggae, salsa, samba, and cumbia.

Contrasted with that of tango, Argentine rock only appeared in the mid-twentieth century. This genre started by imitating Anglo styles of rock and then progressively developed a clear national sound that would be known as "rock nacional" in the 1980s. Having said that, starting with the Beatles' first visit in 1964, it was the British Invasion that would meet the then-rising countercultural youth's desire for imported rock music: from covering bands to originals, including proto-punk and new wave.

By the year 1970, famous rock nacional prefixes such as Sui Géneris were leading Spanish language rock with funk, jazz, and tango treatments that denoted identity. Against dictatorship in the '80s, convulsive bands Sumo and Patricio Rey y sus Redonditos de Ricota were emerging as apolitical rock nacional pioneers with blues, salsa, reggae, and murky existentialism in an Argentinian rhythm.

Thus, when democracy returned in 1983 and borders opened once more, it was during the 1990s that there was even more Anglo influx in manners, for example, grunge rock and Brit-pop. Famous Seattle bands like Nirvana toured Argentina; cover bands emerged; and some of the groups of nacional sang in English for overseas broadcasts. Power was reciprocated, though, as star musician Gustavo Cerati, with emotive guitar solos of his band Soda Stereo, became the first Latin American band to perform in major American venues in the 90's.

As the new millennium approached, global internet sharing quickened bidirectional rock trends once more via file-sharing. In contemporary Argentinian indie styles, one finds, for instance, a portion of global rock à la The Strokes and Arctic Monkeys with blending elements of the local tradition and British pop hooks in the likes of Él Mató A Un Policía Motorizado. Other than rock too, American hip-hop and trap music has gone mainstream and even underground. As one music critic concludes: Thus it may be concluded that globalization has indeed come to Argentine music.

The external motifs were also adopted into rustic folk genres upon movement out of the cities and into the heart of the country, whereby they turned into a local sound. Argentine folk is defined by tender acoustic pop and jubilant country-inflected songs, shy of the tango and rock influences of world cities. But pronounced regional cultural affinities also encouraged the adoption of like styles, Andean in particular.

The chacarera dance with guitar hemiola rhythms, for example, is done in an Argentine style even though the dance occurs throughout the borderlands of Chile and Argentina. Zamba originated in Peru and Bolivia as well also coming into the northwest of Argentina's folklore where the style changed to fit the culture. Pan flutes and charango guitars are the same as used in Indigenous South American cultures. This has resulted in the huge influx of workers from neighboring countries in the past few decades that also accelerated cross-border blending.

Leading folk fusion artists like Horacio Guarany, Mercedes Sosa, and Atahualpa Yupanki made the use of pan-Latin American beats extremely popular though continued using Argentinean themes in the lyrics and the words. More recently still, groups like Onda Vaga keep this cultural heritage alive with high-energy interpretations of Andean wind instruments with Cuban percussion, the Paraguayan harp, the Brazilian cavaquinho, and the Andean charango accompanied by stories from Argentine country life. Within this wide pitch, range could be seen as openness to receiving various kinds of stimuli coming from outside of the culture while still staking the right to own it.

Other such sophisticated musical enclaves can be in the reporters of the classic genre who were trained in European orchestral style, in Argentina, however, transpose the national tunes into global symphonies, giving seeds around the late 19th and then the 20th century.

Major figures, such as Ginastera, Piazzolla, Piantoni, and Guastavino, who were well-known composers, had their formal training in classical composition from performance conservatoires, and their corpus of work deliberately tapped from local musical forms either taken from Argentinean folk songs or from tango dance beats.

It should be noted that it is in the classical forms that Piazzolla changed tango. Having been a pupil of Nadia Boulanger, in Paris, where she was teaching with strict discipline, his classical training enabled him to perform complex and multifaceted symphonies. Breaking a taboo on both sides, he has done such classic works as "Libertango" and "Adiós Nonino," where tango merged with operatic tragedy.

Some of the reasons were political, and they helped in maintaining a national identity within an internationally harmonious orchestration. Composers, between Argentina's one hundred years in 1810 and after a considerable wave of European immigration, have actively tried to maintain tradition in a context of feared erasure of culture while at the same time engaging in the globalist classical movements as a marker of civilization at the time. This was very common, and as time went on and the genres blurred, a matter of national pride for the national artists to adapt the classical Conservatory training, then infuse it with the much-loved genres of Argentine musical genres.

History continues to record efforts towards jazzing, particularly North American horn players and Latin jazz rhythms. Already in the 1920s, innovators of the new tango—bandoneónist Juan de Dios Filiberto and composer Lucio Demare—were influenced by the most popular Cuban and Brazilian styles to begin breaking up the traditional tango instrumentation. American jazz musicians playing in Argentina over the years, among them Cab Calloway and Nat King Cole, also had a role in the development of Argentine musicians in those same decades.

By the avant-gardening 1960s, though, better recorded cross-genre collaborations flourished between bebop jazz musicians and tango legend Astor Piazzolla. After moving to Paris in 1954, Piazolla's classical music enthusiast friend Nadia Boulanger compelled him to develop the tango style he was hiding.

The resultant nuevo tango albums Piazzolla cut with jazz greats pave this style. The summit LP "Summit" with Gerry Mulligan Quartet (Recorded 1974 in Italy) seamlessly improvises over Piazzolla originals adding a chamber string section and smooth saxophone. Called as Talk between the Tangoman and the Saxman, the flow of the musical discussion is evident with ease.

In mid-1967, before going to New York, Piazzolla made an album with alto saxophonist Phil Woods that could be "the first Jazz-Tango fusion album ever recorded in the U.S." Later on, Piazzolla worked with many Brazilian artists such as singer Elis Reginato to further blend the album like "Elis & Tom" in 1974.

These pioneering records assisted to launch the tango fusion upsurge – today continued by contemporary organizations, as the Gotan Project – electro-tango or Alex Krebs Tango Jazz Quartet – California coastside improv. But it goes back to Piazzolla meeting open-minded jazz musicians abroad who were eager to jam with him. Even to date, his legacy continues to be felt through new quartets such as Escalandrum who combine jazz-tango-classical during their touring workshops around the world.

Some good examples, if we consider the history of rock, would be the international stars who travel to Argentina and, the other way around, the domestic performers who act abroad—an unmistakable proof that influence is mutual.

According to folklore, Argentine rockers who in 1964 saw Beatles live in Buenos Aires and later other bands such as Led Zeppelin and Rolling Stones got inspired to form bands in imitation of the Britons. But change brewed by the '70s returned love from visitors where some of its feedbacks are listed and explained as follows; The last star cited when Bowie came to visit in 1997 was Buenos Aires band Los Ratones Paranoicos.

And so, the Californian rock heroes returned the compliment. In a most unlikely collaboration — one that sent Frusciante off to Buenos Aires circa 2009, to record tracks for his solo albums — the Red Hot Chilli Peppers collaborator worked with the legendary guitarist and singer Fito Paez. "When I was 13 and I got my first guitar, I always said that I want to be as good as John Frusciante," Paez said, totally privileged to be working with the musician.

This solidifies, making major international pairings of artists in Argentina, picking up in the 2000s from impromptu backstage jams during concerts to fully sanctioned international recording sessions. Artists as big as legendary Brazilian Gilberto Gil gave performances with Argentine musicians, playing hits from his album of 2010. Alt-rock Vampire Weekend recorded songwriters inspired by Argentina, as did pop-punk Avril Lavigne and Beck guitarist Smokey Hormel.

Besides a one-off show, Omar Rodríguez-López, a Mexican-American guitarist, formed The Mars Volta while living in Buenos Aires for five years and incorporated his Latino roots by jamming with local musicians through lengthy progressive psychedelic rock epics. These connections survived his time with the band as the latter remained intact in the United States afterward. It embodies musical mutual interchange that is set in one location before being disseminated across the world.

On the other hand, over the last century, Argentina has also projected its music further in response to foreign genres infiltrating the nation's culture. The first world stages are soon transferring across continents to nurture new artistic eras—especially given the current advances in technology that drive distribution.

From changing the direction of other Latin American rock bands, and provoking classical symphonies with native concepts to the international branding of the tango dance worldwide with classes from Winnipeg to Tokyo, Argentine music has also been universally influenced both by passion peers and strategic cultural marketing.

It was immigration that formed the basis of the tango fever, sweeping through 1900s Parisian dance floors. It was in the anti-establishment movements of the rebellious 1960s that folk tunes made their appearance. Then came Rock nacional with its volatile dictatorships in neighboring countries. Today, it is through podcasts and music blogs that the fan base of Argentine indie bands is being increased.

It does so through both concrete and intangible channels of commerce—concert tours bringing new sounds, and indirect inspiration resulting in new foreign fusions of source material found at home. Finally, Argentina seems to be ready for the third spot in the rank of countries from Latin America that export musicals.

From the Brothels of port cities to the glamour of Hollywood and beyond in a colorful one-hundred-year sojourn overseas, Argentine music has evolved. It is quite probable that Barisien's audiences fell in love with ballroom dancing to the tunes of tango when visiting Argentine Félix Pellegrini's Parisian gigs and tango dance which is described as "a dance of great charm...of extreme originality."

As soon as WWI emerged, tango schools opened for teaching steps acquired when transported sailors and affluent travelers returned home. Amongst the early birds to take an interest in attempting to incorporate tango in their pieces is the likes of Ravel and Debussy who attempted to do so in piano compositions. It was in the 1930s and 1940s that the first fashionable tango orchestras from Argentina, featuring the bandoneón, started touring Europe: performing in theatres, particularly those theatres just after the Second World War in dire need of cultural visits.

It is in the sensationally performed dramatic tango of global movie stars such as Rita

Hayworth that audiences gained mid-century mass appeal. It is a genre whose study has been taken up by modern-era pop diva Madonna, whose name the avant-garde German electronic group Tangerine Dream made famous, and in whose steps Mikhail Baryshnikov dances with Argentine choreographers.

In addition to the ballroom, global rock got the Argentine effect from Mexico down through Chile and beyond. When democracy ousted dictatorship in 1983, a young Chilean band Los Prisioneros contributed to Argentina's sociopolitical rock for freedom songs in the region. For Mexico in the '80s, another influential Mexican ensemble Caifanes also recorded their version of another classic Sumo song and credited rock nacional fomentation. That translated to Plus singing in Spanish, instead of traditional English rock lingua franca, which appealed to a broader Hispanic population.

In the contemporary broken musical world, today's bands target new audiences through internet services and media such as playlists or blogs. Pitchfork now translates the work of Buenos Aires indie acts such as Usted Señalemelo or 107 Faunos for the benefit of English speakers. Clever music supervisors also include Argentine songs in Netflix show soundtracks to reveal worldwide tune searchers too.

Though measuring influence is a tricky affair, Argentine genres did catalyze artistic movements elsewhere – specifically, more rebellious rock against the dominant culture. Some examples of concrete cooperation with Argentina and abstract inspiration based in the country have touched foreign musicians. As racehorses bred new champions it was the same here that imported musical strains also bred new hybrids sent back overseas.

Except for these, some Argentine artists influenced the style of some non-Argentine performers, together with certain foreign musical genres impregnated with native elements. From Argentine singers and musicians, like Carlos Gardel and Astor Piazzolla, known in Tokyo, to traditional rhythms remixed around the world, people globally have embraced homegrown tunes.

Firstly, he is regarded by the world of jazz, classical, and tango as the person who introduced change in that particular genre. From tacky pop caricature to high intellectual composition, which today is performed in symphony halls across the globe, the dramatic dance improved remarkably under his baton. Libre-tango pieces, for example, are brought into both classical and jazz performances for arranging purposes and now set standards.

Another related classical crossover contemporary of Villa-Lobos was Alberto Ginastera; he also gained international recognition from his combination of modern classical forms with Argentine folk rhythm and instrumentation. As a young man, he was deeply influenced by gaucho guitar concerts around Buenos Aires, which he later combined into his work. His Piano Concerto No. 1 is an outstanding balance between European symphonic and Latina-American rhythm, and it won its place within the repertoires of classical concert pianists worldwide.

Carlos Gardel, the pop vocal singer/songwriter, is perhaps the best example of exported singer/songwriter. Born in 1890 in France but considered one of the most Argentine singers, his elegant, melancholic torch songs enhanced with the tango rhythm are still reminiscent of cafe music around the globe. To this day, karaoke singers all across Asia attempt to mimic his phrasing of Canciónes such as Mi Buenos Aires Querido.

Besides people, even specific music genres incorporated Argentine characteristics. More generally, scholars consider main streams of the relation between Argentina and jazz, such as New Tango (around the early 1960s) when North American jazz men first improvising in tango song forms, Jazz–Tango Fusion after early 1970s when traditional jazz quartets interpretations entering the repertoire. California's West Coast Jazz movement was also embracing counter-culture South American influences throughout the seventies; one crossover LP for example was the Latin-jazz Summit Session between Cal Tjader and Eddie Palmieri, which incorporated pampas textures.

The Argentine genres epitomise globalisation, thoroughly international and themselves. Among the important examples on the worldwide scene, US and European rock and pop together create new hybrid sounds, mixing traditional folkloric rhythms with international music currents. Yet this musical scene remains widely fertile through the hybridization of intercultural fusions, such as tango and electronic music, and between Argentine musicians and foreign musicians in ensembles such as the Gotan Project. But the musical influence of Argentina is much more far-reaching abroad; its sounds are heard far beyond its national borders. Indeed, Argentina's national dance, the tango, travels around the world with dancing schools and events from Paris to Tokyo.

It is through the contributions of Astor Piazzolla, who introduced innovation into the tango, turning the style into a major source of inspiration for jazz and classical composers around the world, that today Argentine rock bands are of world renown, having proceeded to drive the rock scenes throughout Latin America and beyond. It's this two-way conversation—that Argentine music would be incredibly rich as part of the world music tapestry but for its assimilation of influences from the globe.

The Future

Argentinian music remains an important element of Argentine culture to the present day and creates new trends and trends on a historical and traditional basis. In the future, the choice prologues the relations between traditional and new modes of Argentinian music as the genre.

Contemporary music in Argentina is emerging with the progress of new tendencies of music and ways of creating and distributing music through new technologies and social networks.

At the moment the youth culture of Argentina is in an attempt to compose new styles of music which is produced with the themes of Argentina but according to twenty-first-century tastes. For example, Electrotango can be envisioned as music with tango roots being enriched by its orchestral versions, as well as tango being supplemented by electronic kind of dance beats. This does not only aim to maintain the spirit of tango but it also has the goal of getting it as close to the generations of the present time as possible. Bands like Bajofondo Tango Club presented electro tango which fuses elements of tango, milonga, murga, candombe and salsa rhythms accompanied by features of rock, jazz and electronic music.

Another way is the modern folk music opposed by artists like Soledad Pastorutti: she performs folk music that has roots in the northern parts of Argentina with only her voice and brilliant musicians. Continuing, Pastorutti has finally reached the wider circle of the mainstream audience that could rotate as a confirmation that even the modern developments of traditions can draw the interest of the general public.

At the same time, Argentina still has an amazing rock music scene and it actively evolving. Other rock fusion bands include Eruca Sativa and they brought in even more elements, Lula Bertoldi as the lead singer is a powerful feminist. The band includes punk, reggae, cumbia, choros and salsa among them for the performance of their songs.

Rap and hip-hop have also set themselves as exceedingly important and impactful. Since the 1980s, Argentine rap has continued to thrive and even reign with the fast raps of the current Wos, CA7RIEL, and Trueno. These two do lyrics in a way that it is very fast and it may be giving the present-day Argentinian youth, their view on culture and society.

Technology is therefore offering new opportunities in the manner musicians go about creating music, playing it, putting it to tape, distributing it and marketing it. It is to say that such home studio configurations are much less restrictive in terms of creativity and freedom of expression than are the ordinary high-quality studios that allow artists to develop their distinct style and sound more freely.

Other related social sites allow artists to market themselves and their fans across the boundaries of countries. Platforms such as Spotify and YouTube allow connection to points of music distribution to the international market. These actions do not mean that record labels become simple, although they do spur the extremely ferocious struggle for attention on digital interfaces.

Some of the following are; It creates new channels of communication between artists and fans via social media networks. Instagram continues to musicians and is particularly TikTok on making them more creative and risky with brief songs and meme-influenced, viral videos. The existence of such cyber-genres as hyperpop, in which one can mention the participation of artists like Nicky Nicole, evidence of the fact that such settings are involved in the formation of new genres as such.

While technology creates opportunities for upcoming talents in Argentina where they can publish new musical inventions globally, works of the mind need far much better protection. That balance could serve a lot in boosting the awareness of the new musical works originating from Argentina in a way that would not hurt the global platform and performers.

Hence, some measures help in sustaining and preserving the deep generative foundations of the genres and, simultaneously, as new forms come into being there emerges new styles from the old ones.

One thing that should be pointed out is that those advocates are not only preserving but also restoring and disseminating some specific shapes of Argentine musical culture.

At this time, there are fans of the tango genre, defined by a complex beat and the existence of an emotive story or narrative; there are also performers who are concerned with recreating the tango salons of the past and inventing new ones. Certain cultural centres manage to stage traditional dance fairs concerning the true nature of genuine tango and the prospects of further sustainability of this UNESCO-listed endangered cultural heritage.

It is in such formats as the Chamame festival that enable the kind of platform that keeps other genres of traditional music such as the one mentioned above relevant. Teresa Parodi and many other representatives contribute to maintaining the ground of Argentinian folk-popular music, on which experimenters work to expand the genre. Its work in distillate the soul of conventional genres for the young, families and revivalists preserves the link from generations past to the generations to come.

The most enterprising documentation is now collecting material for assembling albums that will graphically show the growth of music in Argentina year by year. National radio stations record a vast amount of sound bites to maintain a chronological record of music categories, commentary and artists' views. Some such organizations like the Barenboim-Said Foundation are toying with the preservation of these cultural artifacts, digitizing them, and making those sources accessible in as many ways as possible, for learning, research or even as scores of new pieces.

What is even more striking is that this kind of clash between the old and the new can be thought of as the struggle between obedience and inspiration.

The fragile balance between freedom and incentive with a guardian of the previous developments is what must be done in Argentina: to protect the soul of the music while letting it evolve is a virtuous goal.

Today's talent builds on such legendary Argentines over centuries who too broadened their horizons — from the tango singer Carlos Gardel who fused European and Latin American tunes early this century or the rock maestro Luis Alberto Spinetta who combined jazz and progressive rock in the seventies. Its effects remain always current and remain to be interpreted as well as adapted.

Similar micro trends at places such as Niceto Club are moderate – the event coordinators make daring electronic musicians perform alongside tango singers and musicians as expected. Tango emerged from cultural roots and internationalized through incorporation but is still cultural; the centennial of tango was marked in 2016 and saw the fire rekindled by fusing tradition with modernity in production.

A young singer Victoria Bernardi shares the documented musical repertory and composes without fear of the concept of creativity. Bernardi also states about the free choice of musical interests that 'it makes the music that is imagined without prejudice. Bernadi's words and views reveal how Argentine music remains liberal and can grow naturally.

Any policy that in any way demeans the creativity of an artisan is pernicious to this mix. New property rules also obstruct the understanding of ordinary noise, where full implementation of intellectual property rules is in force. But enshrining cultural music denies self-promoting stimuli to create new ones at the base. Progress comes from prescribing and developing certain norms that allow for the audacity of innovation while preserving the conventions.

The keys are balance, freedom for creativity and promotion of innovation that preserves what is before these. Some traditions will persist by passing on to the generations and record the direction and policies on how to stand on other people's shoulders to see further.

Argentine music is a rhythmic variation – a combination of layers of soul that grew within generations of Argentines. Anticipated visions with a correct proportion of a traditional and a revolutionary style are enriched and harmonized with progressive fluidity. As for creative musicians, the number of whom is large, they will keep experimenting with the innumerable possible interactions between the traditional musical instrument and the new technologies. Argentinian music has a very long history although it also underwent changes and likewise gradually evolved with the present society yet the tradition still holds strongly at present.

Disclaimer

Everything shared in this book should be considered as educational and informative in nature. The author and publisher shall not be responsible for any loss or damage suffered by any reader directly or indirectly through reading of, reliance on, and use of information that only the author and the publisher know at the time of writing this book.

Some of the suggestions given and the approaches recommended in the book may not be applicable to certain circumstances. The author and the publisher shall not be held responsible for any damages caused as a direct result of the use or non-use of the information presented in this book.

It is understood that readers should not rely on it for professional solicitations such as medical, legal, financial, and other related opinions. If any professional help is needed, then advice of a competent professional person should be taken.

The author and the publisher will not be held responsible for direct, indirect, special, or consequential damages or any other costs whatsoever arising from the use of the information present herein in this book.

About the Author

Maher Asaad Baker (In Arabic: ماهر أسعد بكر), is a Syrian musician, author, journalist, VFX & graphic artist, and director. He was born in Damascus in 1977. He grew up with a dream of being one of the most well-known artists in the world, and he has been working hard to achieve it ever since.

He started his career in 1997 when he was only 20 years old. He had a passion for technology and media, and he taught himself how to develop applications and websites. He also explored various types of media-creating paths, such as music production, graphic design, video editing, animation, and filmmaking. He was not satisfied with just being a consumer of media; he wanted to be a creator of media.

Reading was another source of inspiration for him. He was always surrounded by books as a child, thanks to his father's extensive library. He read books from different genres, topics, and perspectives. He read books for knowledge, for wisdom, for entertainment, for enlightenment. Reading stimulated his imagination and curiosity. Reading also developed his writing skills.

He did not start writing professionally until later in his life, as he was busy with other projects and pursuits. But when he did start writing, he proved himself to be a talented and prolific writer. He wrote articles for various newspapers and magazines on topics such as politics, culture, society, art, technology, and more. He wrote books that were informative and insightful. He wrote books that were creative and captivating. He wrote books that were best-selling and award-winning.

He is most known for his book "How I wrote a million Wikipedia articles", where he shares his experience of being one of the most prolific contributors to the online encyclopedia. He reveals his methods, techniques, strategies, and secrets of writing high-quality articles on any subject in record time. He also discusses the benefits and challenges of being a Wikipedia editor in the age of information overload.

He is also known for his novel "Becoming the man", where he tells the story of a young man who goes through a series of transformations in his life. The novel explores themes such as identity, masculinity, self-discovery, love, loss, and redemption. The novel is based on his journey to becoming who he is today.